Books By Jim R. Rogers

Starts And Stops Along The Way
Sharing Some Stuff
From The Road Most Travel

THE INCREDIBLE IMPORTANCE OF EFFECTIVE PARENTING
Plain Talk About Raising Children
From a Concerned Field Worker

LOOKING AROUND

POEMS BY
JIM R. ROGERS

LOOKING AROUND
Copyright © 2015
Jim R. Rogers

All rights reserved.
This publication may not be reproduced, stored
in a retrieval system, or transmitted in any form:
recording, mechanical, electronic, or photocopy,
without written permission of the publisher.
The only exception is brief quotations
used in book reviews.

Comments: Contact
Jim Rogers at jim@stilllearning.org

ISBN: 978-0-9895042-4-9

Cover/Interior Design: Jim R. Rogers

Prose Press
Pawleys Island,
South Carolina 29585
proseNcons@live.com
www.prosepress.biz

dedication

to those who have much
to those who have little
to possibilities of mixing it up

to sally for listening
for believing
for being

FIRST

1. Turn Our Cheek
2. Now
3. Cozy
4. I'll Know
      (like Ansel did)
5. Crying
6. One
7. And So It Grows
8. Looking Around
9. Hard Stuff
10. Not Today
11. Touched
12. Kelly
13. Special Forces
14. Pre Mature
15. Give Thanks
16. Fore Fathers And Mothers
17. What Shaw Saw
18. Daddy
19. Fixer Upper
20. That Thing
21. Just Lucky I Guess
22. Shiny New Things
23. Will There Be Enough

24 Left Out
25 Real Ones
26 Mac
27 Slowing Down
28 At Risk
29 Used Up
30 Lift And Remove
31 Breathe
32 Not Done
33 Bus Trip

SECOND

34 Stop!
35 Something Funny
36 Disappoint
37 Retreat
38 Imagine
39 Pick One
40 No Fun
41 Left Behind
42 Too Much
43 More Please
44 Me

45 Self Odes
46 50 Years Or More Ago
47 Back When
48 Those Things
49 COD
50 All Over
51 Aging
52 Managing
53 9-11 on 9-12
54 Airports
55 Failures
56 Learning
57 The Dog's In The Closet
58 Still Looking
59 Movies
60 Keep At It
61 Faults
62 Lately

THIRD

63 5 Easy Pieces
      (a tribute to Jack Nicholson)
64 Teacher
65 Finding Me
66 The Dunes

67 Morning
68 Sidelined
69 United
70 Directions
71 Letting Go
72 Trips
73 Solid
74 Mechanic
75 United AME
76 Desire
77 The Edge
78 Cultural Exchange
       (after seeing a tribute band)
79 What Happened
80 Opportunity
81 Questions
82 Fame
83 Hear That
84 Savings Time
85 Look Around Some More
86 Love Yes
87 Modern Music
88 Root Cause
89 Anger
90 Will And Testament
91 Long Enough To Wag

FIRST

Hard boiled eggs are hard for a while until the outer shell breaks and the inside shows

Turn Our Cheek

Tiny spots of greyish orange dot
the places where we look
warm embers clutching each other in
their pits as diseased
breaths blow them into hotter
piles until others see them too,
start to worry if heat will melt the mold escape
as flames to slap us in the face turn our heads,
burn the minds that hoped for better lives
without the struggle to stay upright to walk
the earth proud of who we are and what we're
here to do.

Now

Don't ask me why I'm doing this,
I told you not to ask
I'm doing it, I have the chance
the time the means the wherewithal
the plan is now to do it,
like when I won the hand of her
after years and years pursuing
when that day came I gushed
but didn't know what to do with it.
What can I say that others missed
or does it really matter since
what we need has grown so large I
don't think we can move it. There are
so many good and kind who are
here to make change, they save the creatures
large and small they wrap the needy
in their arms they bring sweet light to
darkened corners of the land, they
offer hope in ways they can. Like lighthouse
beacons they show the way for the
many who are lost, they give their
lives away and at what cost.

So maybe that's the reason I'm
pushed to do this now. So many bad
things close in on us, I feel the need to holler
let the world, the one I know,
have hope that there's tomorrow.

Cozy

Oh look how nice it is in there
festooned by such soft silk,
cushioned from the iron hard seats
where all the others sit,
cocooned in such a way
few sounds can pierce the ear
for sure no cries of loss or pain
from all those way outside.

Just put your feet up
lean back and smile
wait for smoke to clear
it can't be too long a life to wait

For what was in the darkest times
swallowed up by madmen
will cut the ropes of bound-so-tight
move up and through   out beyond with
no one else but those who dare

look back and see what happened then,
what happens now.
Leave it alone, it will fade
it's really gonna be ok
so keep it in a warm and safe
but not too comfy place.

I'll Know

(like Ansel did)

Starting almost first with no
knowledge much to count
moving out with caution since
trust has not been found,
looking for what steps to take
who might lead the way
asking questions not in books with
answers hard to find,
can't expect a lot when
hidden is what's there.
Try, fail again, again with
hopes of some success,
scary places show themselves
along with few warm spots.
Plans are made but disappear much
faster than were made
vantage points that give clear
sight avoid us with alarm.
Not giving up, beyond belief we
dig our blistered fingers in,
feeling burn to find it, not
so sure we can

always looking for the Adams place
the perfect place to stand,
not knowing what to look for but
knowing when it's found.

Crying

Every day I cry.
Some days all day I cry.
Looking back I feel like
I have cried all my life
so far.
A few interruptions of fun, of joy, love
ecstasy, even a laugh
out loud here and there
but so much of my life has been crying
inside for the most part but on some
special days
I would cry outside   only
when the world couldn't see me.
There were so few other times when
someone would be there with me, for me,
letting me, inviting me to cry, all out
full force, emptying myself
with them, sometimes for them, or us
always for us, me being one of us, of us all
so many to cry for
so I do.

One 6

Zillions it will be
if that's a number to be had
elbows touching elbows
noses in ears bodies
so close to each
hardly any space to move.
Ant like busyness darting here
then there lifting much more
than the weight of self,
others too to be helpful, stronger
more polite so all might share the life
lasting so much longer than before.
Tasking every day to make sure
likes and loves hold fast the chain that binds
us all together trying not to see
the link, the weak one that
may break put us in a free fall
tumble into a dirty ditch that was before.
Now we know we can do it, now we know it
can be done. Now we know we have to keep it,
now we know
we can all make one.

And So It Grows

Like a Le Sueur pea it started
tiny, cute, green, oh so round and
tasty, one of just a few side by side
in order, growing well tucked firmly
in the pod protected from direct attack
until the time was right. Growth was
great, pods increased loaded plants were
cropped then peas became the thing as
pods produced more plants became a
field then another then another then
the home, the school, the town, the country
the world came to love peas, grew
more, then more until parking lots
vacant high rises empty rooms welcomed
peas in pods on plants in fields, everybody
buying using up the peas as fast as they
could so more peas were grown
until the peas outnumbered the me's.
That's when we started to wonder.

Looking Around

Our world our planet can
take our breaths away
leave them suspended in
a sweet thin air smooched
often by gentle clouds
sometimes harsh and mean,
loud, harmful then go
away replaced by light and breeze
softer hearts dancing
even alone but with others is best.
The time is short to enjoy,
to embrace, to call our own
even when it isn't but can be
in moments of discovery, of ecstasy,
of belonging, of being human
even though we don't yet blend as
nature does with checks and balance
order of the ways to be in life
so beautiful, so exceptional, so
made for us to keep, not break or
throw away in pieces like
puzzle parts that fit but got misplaced
between seat cushion cracks of our
broken lives which we have to mend
again since this may be our only time and
what a time to miss!

Hard Stuff

Rocks are hard, or supposed to be
some are not for reasons known to some.

    dry concrete is hard but vibrating hammers
with strong men in charge can break it into
tiny pieces which still stay hard,
just not together

    iron is very hard and not much can be done
to change that except the hottest fire known
to man can melt it so it pours into big pots for
remaking into hard somethings.

    steel is hard but I'm not sure why it's not
the same as iron although some people know,
but I don't care.

    teeth, bone seem hard, clay fired well can
be hard for a while then time seeps into joints
small cracks making it weak easier to
fall apart. Hard boiled eggs are hard
for a while until the outer shell breaks and
the inside shows. Math is hard, so is English
language, and Chinese, and Latin, and
homework. New metals are hard platinum,
titanium even tin keeps the rain
out most times.

    Life is hard. Is it supposed to be?

Not Today

Hands slap each other red
mouths release primitive sounds
together creating an audio avalanche that
floods like molten lava into the very
fiber of the creators turning them into
fanatical motivators of those on the field
surrounded by the steel, glass, plastic of
a modern coliseum where today's
gladiators compete for what they are
getting plus heinous amounts of money,
fame and unexpected, unaccepted
responsibility, accountability and self
reliability. Men, women even children vying
for that special place in life that few achieve
and keep. They think it's what they want.
Not many see fewer care that most who
compete are people of color. It's alright, it's
what they can want, it's everything until it's
not. Seeing people being bought and sold used
as pawns between owners, media, even fans
have a say-so, wondering what happens next
how far will it go before someone says
stop!

Touched

There was this song so long ago
still creeps into my psyche.
I ache for it to creep some more
remind me of what almost was,
will be again? Reach Out and Touch Someone
it sang, in a time when connecting was
meaning something again, when we
began to realize how holding hands
hugging hearts could strong our backs
to stand to say how we feel, how we want
union, melding, meshing to help us get
to know the other, washing out avoiding
due to being different in ways that
don't count really, ways that only steal
ourselves while denying possible ones
to know perhaps for the first time.
If it comes again, I'll know. I may not
be here then, but my psyche will feel the hug.

Kelly

Why is she still here,
rolled up in a ball so tight
atrophied with time lost on her.
Years since taste buds felt real food or wine
her favorite, sorry to say. Tubes with
liquid in her side do all the work required
no words have formed from her dry lips
even when they're kissed by
sister, mother, former lovers. By all
and more she's missed.
Why did this happen to one so fair
so much life to go, choices made
were poor they say yet many others
do the same and are still alive today.
Her eyes show signs of knowing
too seldom to be sure
it's painful just to stand and look
it has to be worse for her
yet the aides who tend her say
not so. Lying there with no intent
of teaching as she does
those of us who knew her when
are here now just to learn.

Special Forces

My friend Bob died today.
I knew him pretty well I'd say
better than some I know, even
family spread all over.
To look at him you wouldn't think
there was really much to see,
like a North Dakota Coen
character mild mannered without a clue
but that was not the case at all.
His life was deep indeed with multi
level doings in them that most
would never do. He married twice
each time well with women who
were smart but time away for him
kept pressure on connections
that ached for them to be together
but not for very long.
Two children came one from each
time again kept their love un-grown
he was far across the world in cammies
and desert boots saving lives,
while taking some.

He fought for his beliefs
a special ops pro, one of very few
who daily put his life on line
to find some truths about the ones he
fought against, just to fight them better.
After many years to and fro he came back
home to stay but sadly found he had no
home, it had vanished into air. He took
some time to write a book about his life of
war about his loss of normality with his
children both wives, too. He shared those
times with book store reads, fans began to
follow, a hero to strangers who hugged, who
clapped him back to life. Clever with his
words used as he saw fit, he knew how to
laugh get others in it too. Generous was his
heart, many books he gave for free, but just
as he with smiles had found some hope again,
that heart he gave so freely, changed, but
could not stay. So, it quickly went
away.

Pre Mature 14

His son was barely born he said,
a few ounces only came from her,
so small hard to tell exactly what he was
holding on to the edge of life with
fingers not yet formed enough to
clutch so others grabbed on for him,
made a promise he would not die, to
leave them almost cheering.
love, grit and pure resolve along
with medical wonders put him in
warming ovens adorned with
tubes and pipes that kept the life
pouring in and through the hair like
veins pumping, giving juice to make
him grow for five months there.
He became the boy, the child they
ordered, even with built in delays,
they took him home to start the
trip that would take him where
he surely came to go.

Give Thanks

Push, pull, turn, lift.
Something happens
water comes out
lights turn on
toilets flush
music plays
food stays cold
power comes from some fantasy land
water in a well
or a balled tank above the town
flowing through the ground
up, out in the sink,
wires stretch from pole to pole
through valleys over hiways
surging with stuff that brights the nights,
stores filled with goods we want
some we don't but it's still there
who makes it, what lives do they live
people like us who do such things
build bridges, tunnels, skyscrapers
cars, computers, make things for us
amazing things we can't live without
and we take them for granted.
Shouldn't we say something?

Fore Fathers and Mothers

They fought the king and found usa.
She made a flag they still salute
She healed wounds when no one could
He helped a country set fear aside
He flew airplanes fast and high and he
Made a bomb so many would die
And he made a car so many could ride
Writers of books they defined our paths
She saved the slaves who lived free at last
He built a bridge to connect the divide
And he helped parents teach from their hearts.
A few made wall street roar and rise
Two took charge of our digital lives
Men and women great and small gave
themselves to us all. Those same ones in the
history books we now know lived lives just like
us. Most of us. As husbands and fathers and
mothers and wives, they sucked.

Nobody's perfect.

What Shaw Saw

And then it's time to start,
after being nurtured by some ones
or not, after some kind of getting smarter
or not, before we do anything of worth at all
we start. Write and speak and search and
research then test and try and bump into walls
of others' truths, we stagger making mistakes,
fools of selves then after so much work, we
progress, baby steps first then larger and larger
until we get there seeing something for the first
time we thought we always did, knowing now
we didn't.

Daddy 18

Admired by town and church and rotary too,
so many looked to him for reason, skills to get
things done with little dysfunction from much
hard work, at times in shifts by neighbor teams
who cared. Quiet and wise, bone-deep honest,
not knowing how much it was wanted by
those who yearned to be so like him,
successful, fair, never rough, and kind.
Had to be a man who knew himself, confident,
sure of it all yet he was not always, rather
searching for what he wasn't sure since he had
never asked before, his spirit seemed content.
Missing something, he ached in silence never
really knowing love missed him, and he it, only
as it was from mother and she was never
sure herself.
He wanted more. He wanted to have. He
wanted to give. I knew it. At last. He asked.
When I was thirty four I helped him learn
to hug.

Fixer Upper

It leapt off the wall at me
bonked me square between the eyes.
Don't know why I didn't see it coming
yes I do, I wasn't looking.
While it was happening I was somewhere else
in my mind, in my head doing other things.
Acclaim was out there I knew it was
I pursued it without much thinking
not seeing how the paint was fading,
making peeled chips leap in anger.

Didn't feel the floor boards sagging
squeaking under hurried steps,
or the wall where pictures hung
the glass the frames were dulled by dust,
dated bathroom toilet water gurgled
finding little room to exit,
leaks gave texture to the cabinets
underneath the sink, roaches were free range
types going where they pleased,
window caulking as brittle thin ice
let in the wind, rain and critters,
shower mat suction cups held a suck no more,

towels, sheets and pillow cases so
frayed, only seldom guests would wink behind
my back knowing things like that were not
concerns for me, since I was
busy living life not to notice what
was passing into past.

How short the time is left to care for all
that needs some help, needs some fixing up.
For me to even stop to see my face reflected in
the milky glass, yellow teeth sure signs of no
attention. Too late I'm sure to make amends
for neglect of heart and home
I sit alone in a tattered chair staring
at the wall staring back at me, blaming
me for all, and of course, I know it.

That Thing

Just look at it...standing there
looking back at me
it thinks it's boss and
controls what's next
how foolish it can be.
It never met me before
knows nothing of my life
who I was who I am and
who I plan to be
knows not the depth of courage
nor supports surrounding me
knows not that I have fish to fry
and other things to do
knows not that I have loves to tend
discoveries to reveal
a life so fully just to live
moments I will cherish
as long as I am here
I plan for that to be
for some time yet to come.
It cannot scare me from my stance
It cannot see that I am free from
thoughts to walk a path of any misery.
So butt out you who thinks you're cool
leave my days alone go play in someone
else's life I have to get back home.

Just Lucky I Guess

Never worry about food to eat,
clothes to wear, even special treats.
Selection made the choice for some
they dropped in place just right.
Early days great care was there
to make the moves prescribed
by those in roles who make the rules
to set the steps to take.
Do this task first then follow suit
stay in line do what they say
that school will be the one
to grow your brain
to lead you to the job
they're holding till it's time.

   He did and look at him
he's done quite well you see, a fancy car
a house so grand, trimmings all abound
not much left to want
a treasure chest quite full of things
all bought on line or from the store.
But wait, the love that was to be
a hug, a touch, a close connection just not

found lonely times are what they live,
absent from some care
they numbly go with all they have
but little they can feel.
Don't be sorry for them though.
They're the lucky ones
you know.

Shiny New Things

Having something now that never was before
baffles as excites, numbs the senses for a while
slowly waking up to what is now real but not
knowing exactly how it goes, what to say, who
to be when faced with making moves doing
what's required.

Windows open to fresh breezes that cool hates
and fears rooted in the past. Slammed back
shut fast loud hard that's not the way to do it.
What to do with it, fast growth into big jobs
some stumbling as they go. Educate, train at
work, practice days on end. Celebrity comes,
some so too soon looking for someone to lead,
to step up, to show the way, how to mix with
grown up minds spent in years of knowing.
No foundation just demeaned,
got to get out of here.

Riches new come too fast cloud the head
harden the heart as angry voices rise to cover
up the lack perhaps, what too fast does to
chance, it's not to change it's just too hard to
do. The best is all there is for now, so keep it
where it is.

Will There Be Enough 23

For all that's growing now
for all that seems so lost
an instant world pulls up her skirt
then drops his pants
to show it all any time of day or night
in any place almost.
No shame it seems in wanting more
or not wanting what we have
it's mine, no it's mine and you can't have it now
when then and how much. It can't go on like
this. Older wiser ones who felt their lives were
good sit lonely now with no love touch nor
anyone to say I miss you I
wish we had more time
time for what, more of this,
more of what we never thought
could be, what is wasting, torn apart,
what we had and may never find again.

Yet hope is there it has a smell, a taste,
a feel of some who care
who want to stitch it up again.
Young ones not yet deformed

not only think of self but
more of them and those to come
with no fore thoughts about it all
uncolored by the dark
they will clean the spots, start all over
if wise un-rotted aging minds
will just give them a chance.

Left Out 24

No one should be left out
No one.
It's here for all of us
many don't get what they need
labeled MIL, Missing in Life.
And they feel like shit.
Like nobody. Not seen, not heard, not present
or accounted for. So they do things
what they need to do to be here to tell them
they are alive to let us know they are
makes them feel special to get noticed.
Toddlers start it and we hear them
from then on the acts are more and so oh my!
Clothes. Look at things they wear. We do.
They want us to. Nobodies with 'tudes that say
"I'm here. See me!" Objets d'art stuck through
in/out ears, noses, tongues, belly buttons and
clits. I don't know how that works.
Motorcycles make dragon roars, belch fire and
smoke with riders' butt close partners tattooed
from nip to toe, big wheel trucks take so much
space leaving others none "look at us who live
so wild so different you cannot follow, you
on the path of doing, being, having, behaving,
keeping. We are the special ones. We are not
in your line. We have our own."

Real Ones

Looks of disgust from others
who are above them in every way,
they think. Oh so loud, crude
most always rude, with beer bellies
pants worn out way too low
tee shirts with art in-the-face
jokes are bad, taste the same.
Women are tough some quite pretty
under it all, the make-up, the extra hair
the fingernail weapons white as snow
sharp as icecycles just as cold.

   And in some miraculous way They take the
days as they come, if bad, ok, if good, better.
They stay busy with something anything not
to think too much since when they do, stuff
barges in, causes pain confusion frustration and
reflection on what was lost, never found and
will not be there again, if ever, who they are not
never will be.
And yet
When something happens to their town,
their neighbors, their country, their schools,
they molt into another gear, a place those

others never reach. They rush to give their
help, their courage, their strength to pull debris
from covered bodies, to drag almost victims
from rushing flood waters, to warn about the
dangers, to protect from looters, to carry the
hurt to safety or to treatment. They are our
heroes. The real ones. You don't see them
taking credit on the news as eager reporters
ask how do you feel. If one answers it's usually
with a bewildered look and a how the hell do
you think I feel? They are our bad times friends.
We wouldn't invite them over to the house for
a cook out, but we could owe them our lives.
Most times not thanked, or appreciated being
some of the earth's salt, spoken about in songs
and poems. That's why they're them.

Mac

Red and yellow and green and just a touch of
blue for his eyes.
He hangs from the rafter where
he's been for years,
under the dust.
Still seems happy
more so when the heat comes on
and gives him a twirl. Play time.
We see him smiling as he spins and watches
us kiss good morning
put on our clothes. He doesn't seem to mind
who we have become.
Like us.

Slowing Down

On the way to silence
allows all those thoughts busyness has kept at
bay to close in.
Come to a complete halt
And it all rushes in like the dam burst
floods the mind, then the heart
then the soul.
All those put away memories,
plans made, hurts them and me, sadness
seeped in, lost directions that were a life.
Now the young, more busy than one could ever
be with little time to think about thinking
About planning
Finding purpose
Building selves into people we can like
live with
die with and trust
to leave something behind.
Something better than we left for them.

At Risk

Looking around it's all of us
from the beginning a dice roll, not knowing
who they are what they do or will do   ever
some know or think they do and some just
shrug about what it takes to make a world so
safe. No one is concerned no one worries no
one looks over shoulders or runs in the dark
away from the boogies that lurk, pounce and
steal the life the love, the should be, the ought
to be, the why can't it be for me, for them, at
least the ones who have no say so, no sense of
what it is what it was or can be.
Who will hold their hands help them cross
the street walk them to a place where the sun
can shine some time, where wounds are closed
where there can be smiles as gifts,
that place so plainly promised
to some.

Used Up

Incredible the way the word is used
so many ways now for any and every one,
from teens and their BFFs, parents and their
bills, accountants and their numbers, lovers
and their loves, dancers and their dance,
doctors and their ills, reviewers and their plays,
anchors and their news, mothers and their
babes, homeless and their lives, players and
their teams, front men and their bands, agents
and their stars, teachers and their schools,
politicians and their plights, composers and
their movements, golfers and their game.
Incredible.
The impact has gone, used up by being used.
What now, when it truly is   Incredible.
What's left for Shakespeare and Conroy
What's left to be incredible.
Try awesome.
Too late.

Lift And Remove   30

That's what it's called at the surgery shop.
Too much was there to bear, blurred
the vision and the vanity of one so sure
there was more, so much that he was missing
not seeing above around through under it all
for understanding of what it took to get the
looks the applause, the best reviews one could
give or get. It was just too much, too heavy
laden on what he could see and
what he could not.
He just heard about the process so he found
the ones to make it happen and it did and
it didn't help a bit.

Breathe

It's raining.
Like it was four years ago today.
Not heavy, can't-see-a-damn-thing rain, but
soft, dense, then like a very wet fog, tricky
pretty but it deceives.
Stealth puddles in low places
that treat deep tread tires like glass
snow sleds on a thick pond of ice.
Hydroplaning.
The heavy grandpa van lifted off the road
sailed across the middle grass aiming toward
the other side four lanes filled with more on
their way to someone else
unaware we were there. She took charge
turned the wheel and touched the brake just so
the metal rail kept us straight and upright and
stopped.
Shit. Oh shit, we said and looked for blood or
break. There was none.
Shattered windshield, totaled car and us
without a scratch that we could see that day.

It's raining. Like it was four years ago. And
We are here. To remember to feel
thank someone and breathe.

Not Done

How sad the days that pull us down deep
inside ourselves. Time is short,
think not to waste it in the past where
what was done is done
of use, only if you can

Of course
there's hurt
there's life that's missing
will always be

And you want him/her/it back.
But that can't happen except in dreams, in
thought, in heart
those unique memories filling that place
you can visit any time when you need it most.
They get even more precious as the need to
have them happens less and less but remains
powerful still.
There's more.

Bus Trip

rumbling down the highway in early days
hot, dusty, close to each other for the ride but
divided when the chance is found.
Riding on just six then, grown to many more,
like so much else to carry the load. Gets too
jumbled with doors open and open again to
those from country roads and city streets
from ditches of lost hope, families dying in
groups from less, or more than there might be
somewhere else but yet to find, if ever, with no
hi tek not even low.
Seats filled with strangers who stay the way
they want or riding partners linked for life or
while it lasts, as they get off at each stop to
see what's there, if it fits, if it gives or takes
or maybe both while the big bus pulls away
leaving behind those who wait too long
waiting for the band to play
you're home.

SECOND

I'm just going to tear off a tiny corner and snuggle under the covers until it all slows away.

Stop !

Try stopping, everything.
Sit, stand, lay down, stop thinking
stop feeling stop wanting stop hating stop
loving just stop. Stop time. It happens. Then
time runs out, stuff rushes in, keeps rushing,
we can't keep it out, it lives here
grows like briars gone wild as they do.
Meditate on that, about nothing.
You can't do it. I dare you.
You can't keep it out, it doesn't matter what
you want. And there is no time or way to
reflect to remember to appreciate.
There is feigned silence the wrong kind of
silence, the grieving kind, the lost kind
the don't know what to say kind,
the don't know what this means kind,
the keep trying to keep it out so you won't
have to plan or go or do or be and just keep
trying, kind.

Something Funny

Write something funny, they said.
What funny. Funny strange? Plenty of that.
Funny ha, some of that and strange too.
What's funny to me may not be to you
some think what politicians do is funny,
strange and ha. Some think governments, even
presidents are funny, they are, strange and ha.
Some see funny in an NRA nut
holding a weapon over his head defying those
who would take it away. Funny to me is the
wide chasm between those who laugh at those
who cry. I see late night jon and stephen make
such funny ha and funny strange, their sheep
just hoot and holler fall off their chairs as do I.
I also weep, wring my hands over the other side
which is not funny not strange, not ha, but sad
to me.
Not to them but, right. We, the others, are the
funny strange, the ha and wrong.
Very wrong. I think that's funny.

Disappoint

No days go by without some sadness
short or forever, what was expected, hoped for,
looked forward to, knew it would happen just
the way we thought.
We work at not wanting too much
yet we do, we ask for just the right amount we
deserve. At the pick up door it's slammed in
our face just as we reach out to take what we
heard was offered, what we thought everybody
could have
a good day's work, someone to love who
returns it, a chance to grow to find a way to
get from here to there without much loss,
without much pain, without much anger, yet
we stand numb staring out yonder down the
road wondering what happened and why to
me, always me.

Retreat

She and me we made it nice
a retreat for us alone.
So few come so we noticed
it's just another place to them retro and
boring. Not to us, clearing, raking, cutting,
pruning, planting.
She made flowers bloom their best, I know
they liked her touch   I did
and fairy gardens fairies would admire
feeders for birds who came to dine
passed the word and others came
she always kept them filled.

Holes for plants and handy man things
building fences to keep us safe from curious
eyes. Ease of walk on thin layers of needles
released from tall pines under trees rich with
green in summer but no grass to keep.

Viewed from the street twinkilie lights
sparsely posted like sentries far from gullies
and crevices of city life where years were spent
in tough pursuit on rocky paths to

what seemed dead ends with no idea that
this would be where it really stops at last.
Birds at windows, squirrels running on vines
outsmarting the high tech feeders for only a
while. It didn't work for me either so this is
perfect, maybe heaven.

Imagine

Match sticks made my first known path
big fat wooden ones from the cardboard red
white and blue box, the center drawer that
slid in and out. My daddy would render them
harmless fire makers, I would push them
ever so close to each other pointed in definite
directions from here to there, through scary
twig forests, over mud-filled rivers, such boy-
made dangers with scrap wood walls to help
keep me safe from play-like monsters, to help
me know where I was supposed to go, where
I had been. My stick men walked, my soldier
troop marched my cars rumbled back and
forth more often than not disturbing the match
board order but that was half the fun putting
it back together, loving the stories I played
and lived on the dirt floor of the open garage
attached to our simple home in our
simple town where we lived a simple life so
long ago.

Pick One

We all need a road
doesn't have to be straight,
best not to be but for sure solid grounding
is good, makes it weather absorbent and
resilient. Where is the road going
is there a final destination, do I travel there
alone. Who built it, does it have an end
are there detours or does it go where it's
going and no one knows but it and it ain't
talking. Strange fun to find out more about me
something else added to the list of things to do,
side roads to explore, unknown talents to tap.
Could I have wasted all this time developing
a gift that didn't keep on giving
that was never even mine, that devolved into a
cesspool of regret...
did I stay on that road too long,
made ruts so deep,
I can't climb out.

No Fun

Choices abundant to make every minute of
every single day all life long, decisions about
it all, everything. For good, for bad but not
knowing either until later maybe.
This will do that, might cause that
this will ban pain, that will make us fat
this will taste so good you'll look so much
better. She will kiss then tell and make your
life hell, oh, take this pill if you feel that way.
Read this book, ask this doc, take this class,
get that job, there's a choice of doing, one for
being and so much more. Decisions to choose
or choose decisions or just say fuck it all!
Hey, don't put that stuff in your body
don't sit in one place too long and don't watch
the TV it will kill you in place. You know
you're a racist you're a left wing nut.

Paying attention to it all can cause anxiety (a
bit) run you down, maybe run you over leaving
tire marks in a squishy brain that make your
life miserable ... or ... go ahead, do it all,

let the flood of advice wash over you clean you
out clean you up
you could live well, confusing, healthy
boring, no fun, bland, detached, conflicting
maybe all that's around, all that, for a long time.
Why?

Left Behind

The day they come, calm organized
planned smiles all around or
chaos, cries anger pain blame
regret with frowns and yells.
They can't remember or can they and
know to be thankful or remorseful for
the place they land. Then details of daily caring
or not sacrifices of self, career, future, desire all
put on shelves to best care for them some say,
others see it as choice, destiny, goal to bring
them life the best that there can be paying
the way, paving the way, supporting the falls,
cheering the wins, watching them grow into
what they will be and then on to more alone
remembering or forgetting where they came
from who was there doing what. Some or no
gratitude from them to them, no thanks for
sharing at least not now. Wait until there's
nothing left.

Too Much

Overwhelming comes to mind, then
like estranged in-laws with
baggage on their backs
take the guest room, growing roots
tentacles attaching to synapses
charging with currents too strong for the fuse
so it blows!
The page called life is way too large
all kinds of colors and ways of being, named
places wanting and not wanting to be
texts in multiple words longer than a NYT
piece, digging deeper deeper into the whys, the
hows, the whats, so many what ifs, the so what
nows.

I'm just going to tear off a tiny corner and
snuggle under the covers
until it all slows away.

More Please

Wayne and Clara would tag along too
sometimes to that great play area that was
granddaddy Bell's dairy farm.   We were
squirted with cow's milk when we got in the
way, we learned that cow feed didn't taste that
bad.

A full day of play at the big ditch gone, we
snuck a handful of feed, followed that with a
rabbit tobacco cigarette or two. Brave with
good timing we'd steal an asthma cigarette
from grandma Bell's supply, tiny as it was
she blamed us later telling how bad we were
cutting her life short. Yesterday riding down
our country road I remembered more things,
we chewed weed   sourgrass weed. Could have
killed us. One of many could haves.

We climbed high trees higher than allowed,
jumped down from hay lofts like supermen
would, capeless, bouncing on our hands, heads
then the butts somersaulting, but just one
broke a finger then a leg.

Snakes slid into our cardboard fort when
we slept out at night, we laughed and stifled
giggles as we looked at magazines touched
ourselves got scared that we made it come
out as we did, not knowing it should. That
happened a lot. We made things happen not
knowing they would, we did wide eyed young
things not knowing we should. When daddy
found out, he knew and sorta smiled.

Times were good then when some people
cared. We got through childhood somehow.
I'm counting on more somehow.

Me

Trying to get to me
was
is
will be
a struggle
no one wants to know me
no one asks who I am
no one seems to care
yet I do since I don't.
The wanting makes me burn inside
which moves me to think about, look into,
question, agree or not, wonder if it's this one
or that one
the one I want to be, the one I can be
or the one I can't be and find that out too late
to notice.

Self Odes

A ribbon was cut for a new one today
solid brick fortress-like with rooms for learners
sent by parents hoping for futures to pay them
back. It has a name for the generous giver
making it loud and clear he could.

Last week another monument for sports was
launched where the strong, the brave get
cheers mostly for feats performed for crowds
who pay and give as did the donor whose name
is large, can't be missed.

Corporate gifts abound for events grants to
move forward good things already growing
giving back to those who have some, enough to
matter making sure that papers TV NPR know
who they are just in case someone forgets.

The orgs, for and non, work hard for some but
some lose track of what was going to be
not for them but more for me since I don't have
so much myself and now's the chance to

change, see how I can get make my claim / give
it a name. Mine.

Foundations top the list of odes with givers
who banked it all to spread for those who meet
the need, directed by a staff or two who choose
for reasons known to them, while mystery
holds for those left out, those down the street...
not a mile away...the rest in need of many
things, looking for odes to the many
who don't need them
who may just want to share
who don't care who knows their names.

5o Years Or More Ago

Ten year old eyes see things in their own way
like the day the white sheets came to town,
hid their faces in cone hats with holes for eyes,
cursing mouths, looking like soldiers from the
crusades or something seen in a school book or
an old timey picture show.

They rode in cars and on them hanging from
the bumpers fenders and in those days running
boards, hundreds of them it seemed, toting
rifles held above their heads and yelled stuff
that ten year old ears had never heard, lots of
people on the sides some cheering some not,
but scared, anxious standing in the streets on
the railroad tracks that ran through the center
that divided more ways than one or two.

Their ten year old eyes looked to each other
afraid, they held hands as they backed away
running hiding before anyone could see that
they were friends, no matter who said what
or did what or burned Jesus crosses in the
newspaper man's yard at night to scare him the
way they tried to scare everybody. He stood
tall and so did they but they were just children
colored and white and they were only ten.

Back When

You don't know me, how could you
you were not there when I was born
in that tiny bedroom with the help of the
family doctor who called my mother by her
name and held her hand for comfort.

You didn't sleep with my brother and me in the
twin beds with no heat as we always raced to
the duo therm in the bigger room and had all
the windows wide in summer long before auto
cool spoiled us.

You didn't watch me grow, playing in the
woods, freshly plowed fields with clumps for
chunking, safely raised by the whole town but
mostly by a warm loving mother and a firm
honest dad.

You don't know how my early years helped me
trust, believe in honor and friendships how I
worked hard to be non-judging, accepting of
all who were different in many ways. You were
not there to see me fail miserably at most of

those efforts. You didn't see me try to stand alone, then join, get in line and catch the cadence.

You didn't see me as loyal church goer believer in a Methodist God trying to be the good boy everybody thought I was, teaching the word when I could giving the choir my angel voice.

You don't know how little I learned from my father about being one although he was as good as he could be. There were no grandparents to give wise counsel to what was coming since it had come and gone for most of them.

You would be surprised at how little I knew about girls, love and relationships, saving myself as required for my first wife, later giving all I could to the other two.

You weren't there when the children came as we trialed and errored with little knowledge,

poor modeling, working hard moving up,
leaving behind the love it took to stay together
and like each other for life.

Call it neglect. Some do. Even abuse. Scarce
time for each, it was simple ignorance about
what was needed, what would be. Some say
I've made a mess, can't go back and change it.
That is true. I did just that. I would if I could
but I can't. Who can.

You weren't there to help me then. It was
mine to live, decisions to make, with decision
making tools for fools.

It was my life to live. It only happens once we
have this chance. This one chance. Then what.
How else to do it? How do we know until we
get to where it hides and seek.
I screwed up. We all screw up. In our own
ways. There is no perfect, there is no right
way, wrong way, this way, their way, my way,
your way.

It's all ways. It stays always.
We never know that when we start. Do we.
What would you have told me?
Do you know?
How could you?
You weren't there.

Those Things

They show those things
those awful things of the past
infants wrapped in stinky blankets
hanging on a peg, put away in homes with
a bowl per day. Deep red cuts across black
backs for learning how to read. Near naked
skeletons staring into space being stored in
strange places that will make them well, more
likely dumb them at the end. White and native
scalps hanging from spears dripping the same
color blood on a ground claimed by both. Real
skeletons in cloth shreds stacked in, on rows
from cleansing showers, they said ready for the
big hole. Starving people in far off lands and
right down the street. Why do they show all
those things over and over and over.
So we will know them. So we will not forget.
So they will never happen again. Learning by
not doing what has been done.

COD

It's out there
One is waiting for me
looking to pounce on/in and take me away.
Which one
So many could
No signs yet
Many seeds sowed
Who they were, what they had
What I did and did not
All sets it up
MD's and meds stall it all
a pill for this
a pill for that.
One will break through
One will take me down
Please not pain
Please not long
In sleep is best
Oh, god, not a teenage driver!

All Over

It's not very different
not so much unique more alike than not
life is out there everywhere
like kudzu it's
all over

The childhood was a good one
but only for a while
then adolescence barged right in
just like that
all over

The parents had a good thing going
when the babies first were born
as time went on they grew up
oh oh it's
all over

Relationships are hard at best
even when there's love
shoulds and coulds get in the way
oops it's
all over

Good careers are rare indeed
but then there are successes
until new knowledge ages one
wake up it's
all over

Looking out, there's so much
that really needs some changing
that's what many folks are saying
just listen, it's
all over

Climate worries, war and strife
disharmony 'mongst the humans
at the top of most concerns
they say it's
all over

If our planet is to survive
it will take us all to love it
if we stay the way we are
no doubt then, it's
all over.

Aging

Aging they say is all in your head.
That's true
Except the parts that are in
your knees
your hips
your joints
and assorted
other parts where
aches and pains
hang out and
greet you daily
just to remind you
and keep your head
from getting
too lonely.

Managing

Here it comes again
Another day to manage
To get through
Not old yet, but broken
No wind, no energy
Lost Love Care Interest
In him by him and others, all others
His fat slid down
Sucked up his penis
His knees can barely hold him up
His toenails unattended, he cannot see them
He has no one who helps.
Disease and more
Leave him without his favorite thing to do
Shag, the beach dance
His only love
Lost forever.
But
He manages.
Most of us do.

9-11 on 9-12

Yesterday came and
went again
Years now since they blew
down the buildings
Memories vary feelings vary
some Sad Glad Mad
Hate them for what they did
Love them for what they
didn't know
As in what they were doing
Mis guided Missing something
never had
Always wanted
would never get
Until now
Hard to forget
For some.

Airports

People watching.
Sitting in the airport, nothing left to read
No ear bud iPhone iPad iAnything but I
Just me and myself
thinking, reflecting, looking
at the masses, all so different.
Each is each and single
short and tall, hair and bald
fat and thin, pale and colors mix.
Some with no chin, some with many
Most so plain
Few overdone
Twosomes too,
one ahead or behind
fast pace like late
or slow I can't go.
Most of us are not attractive
maybe 5 in 20 could catch the eye
of perhaps the other 5.

Failures

We call efforts that didn't make it
Dreams that didn't find a life
Ideals left to wander
Directions that went astray
Relationships that dried up
Respect that was punctured with holes
And yet
We made it here to a place that's right
To the place that was waiting for us to arrive
Mistakes.
We had some
But had we not...
We would not be here now
And we are, and happy
So
Who has failed.

Learning

Start out small
Inch by inch
Pound by pound
We go we grow into life
Expecting Good Happy Success
And
We get some, maybe lots
Maybe just a little, if any at all
We embrace
We push away
We look ahead
We remember
We give
We take
We cry
We laugh
And in it all
We learn
All life long.

The Dog's In The Closet

The first warning of something bad coming
long before human ears could
hear the boomers
before eyes could see the rain
streaks of sky fire.
Done without much to-do, silently creeping
not to be noticed, not to be the only one
missed when things
got rough.
After years
we used it for more,
when things got rough
things we'd rather miss
not wanting to talk about
hear about
see happening.
Instead
forewarned
Something bad's coming
The dog's in the closet.

Still Looking

Who gets compliments anymore
Used to be
Handsome, Pretty, Virile
Great shape
So young
Movie star
Leading man, Woman
Wear that well
Such fashion.
Now we know
When we hear one coming
Oh look at you, you look great,
Being nice
Not sincere
But staying
Humble
As before
Responding with
What, oh
This old thing?

Movies

have always been favorites
Saturday afternoon horse operas
cartoons, short subjects, previews
right through the years
to computer generations of
Avatars and
Transformers
and walking dead zombies
and blood sucking vampires.
So many movies
warped my sense of time.
Pieces of lives lived in scenes
sewed together with
music
effects
explosions
created unreal life lines
hiding the worst.
The days between
are the hardest to take.

Keep At It

Skin thins wrinkles wrinkle
Get deeper then multiply
Feet unsure slightly now
Minor bumps
Joints ache
Ears strain to hear
Eyes squint to see
Teeth turn colors if they stay
Gait slows down
Thinking takes longer
Uncle Sam's meds arrive
Chairs that lift, sometimes walkers
Things that say Old
How can it be?
My self, Still here
My heart, Still young
Life
Still full
Ready for more!

Faults

He never touched us right,
he never listened, too.
We never heard anything that sounded like
love at all. But he paid the bills and there was
food, a roof, Goodwill clothes. He worked
three jobs at least. She said she loved him.
In spite of it.
She stayed so long. For us. Then left.
For good. For her.
She wouldn't let him see her love us. We saw it
in her eyes heard it in her voice.
We knew it and that took us through.
Almost to where we are.
We did the rest ourselves. Still hoping to find,
what? When we find it, we'll know. Maybe.

The town loved them both. They were fine
citizens who did a lot for all. The church,
the homeless, the needy, the children who
belonged to others. Whenever we shared,
we heard it from our friends, their mothers,
fathers, deacons, policemen, aunts and uncles,
grandparents too,
well, honey, we all have our faults.

Lately

Been reading about the God particle
that teentsie weentsie no see'um
that has Footprints and Shadows
and can hold Things and People together
and also let them go
but let them all stay
side by side each into each
like Trees to Planks and Rocking Chairs
Boys to Men and
Girls to Women
and other creatures to Others
to becoming Something else

But still

Be Here
and
Whole
and
Complete.

THIRD

Sadness covers the living with havings much too small to measure.

5 Easy Pieces
(a tribute to Jack Nicholson)

She's everywhere
In the drug store
At Hardees and Bojangles
In the grocery deli
At the doc's office
She takes my movie ticket
At breakfast there are many
The hospital has a few
Airplanes too
Big box check outs for sure
It seems to be just old folks
males and females both
There must be a school she attends
To learn just how it works
She means well
that's for sure
But I always want to say
unless you want to bed me

don't call me honey

Teacher

Mrs. Woody. Yes, Mrs. Not Ms. Not Dr. Not
Beth. But Mrs. Pronounced then and there
Mizriz. In our small school in our small town,
southern, isolated nice undereducated folks
who seemed content.
Church folks. 2 or 3 Methodists even.
Similar, routine, order. We all did pretty much
the same things everyday. Every year.
Not Mizriz Woody. She broke out from
somewhere else and came to us.
She talked about those places
of adventure, fun, work, discovery,
finding new ways to think, to learn, to grow.
She made it sound so much better
than what I had. What any of us had.
So when the time came, I broke out and lived a
full life away from where I was.
I owed a lot to Mizriz Woody and
before she died
I came home and told her so.

Finding Me

Before I was a woman I was a man
all that men were then, almost.
I tried to find my place with them
manly sports, locker room couture
exchanging quick drags, bad words bad jokes
about Girls Parents Teachers
Sissies then, queers, now gay
Jews and Blacks... Colored then
And Old Folks and Reetards and anybody else
different. Wetbacks, Slopes, you name it, they
did. We were branded ignorants
with no one to guide us better.

But I didn't brand.
I liked to talk about heart things and
listen and not criticize but find the good
I cried and men never cried
they kept it all inside covered.

Not me. I let it out, I cared
got shunned got joked about
except by the girls, and the teachers and my
Mother, then my wife who let me be me.
She called me one of them
Wasn't that odd. Back then
When I was a boy
Before I became a woman.

The Dunes

Solitude.
In it but not alone,
multi-sized people as to levels reached
like colony ants crawling determined
up and down in and out of mountains
canyons of nothing but sand, high, wide, long,
and old, of many colors timed so by sun and
clouds. Seekers seeking, sliders sliding, jumpers
jumping, show-offs running
grinning.

I found my peak too close to the edge
crept back to watch from below
way below, at the foot where water rarely
flows but relics of rushing, tumbling,
smoothing, drying, blowing remain, some on
top waiting for an eye to catch pick up take
home for the table in the den.

On the what-was river bank I am taken
by the stark white aspen surrounding a place
where long-ago people *had* to dwell sing songs,
tell stories and bathe in the warmth of the fire
being together in life.

Turning around I see my foot prints left behind, only mine, feeling special but knowing that so many had stepped there before.

A strange, skeletal weed tumbles against my leg a few scattered used-to-be trees now stripped of everything but their time-created deepest layer of beauty beckon me to rest. I sit on one
                      and cry

There is nothing else I *can* do.

Morning

First check obits
who's there? who's not?
Not me. Made it another day.
So many have so much
Long details
Everything they ever did
Awards
Honors
Successes
No failures
just this one, if you can call it that.
Wondering now
mine won't be that much
very little really
Less is more?
Life is not measured
by the length of the
obit.
Is it?

Sidelined

Where we live has many roads
Some have sidewalks others none
All have sides of sorts
Sides of paths, sides of streets
where trucks load up on regular days
pick it up haul it away.
Stacked shit on the side by the sides
discarded, used up, purpose served,
tables for snacks and ash trays
lamps that kept the dark away
chest of drawers without the drawers
at Christmas, trees forlorn and dry with missed
balls still hanging for squirrels to play. Broken
worn out, useless things
chairs, beds, junk not good enough
for yard sales

But

Someone else will pick it up use it once again.
New purpose found for just a while,

look some more what else is there,
pruning scraps make way for new,

remains of what had grown so well
cut away from long life roots
taken for the young to be someday
like other things discarded too
fulfilled complete finished
left by the side of the road
no more use for them.

United

We sit so close in planes these days
unless we have the bucks for more
metal tubes with cloth and plastic
chairs have shrunk as prices grow.
We never speak not even when we touch
oh, sorry.
If we are to combine, to be unified
we're a long way from it
we have much work to do.
Saying good morning to strangers
gets a grunt if that
no one wants to talk
afraid of being bored too long
no one wants to hear, who cares about you?
Certainly not the plane people.
After years of hearing safety things
things so serious are silly now
smiles and comfort left long ago with
seat cushion is your flotation device,
remove it, take it with you. Really?
Closest exit may be behind you
doors can be used as rafts!
Minutia details of futile rote, breathless

announcements in a race, all about the dangers
real and not so much.
Who will remember when the time comes?
What was that twenty third psalm
Oh yes no food service.
Wanna bite?

Directions

Men won't ask for them
True enough. In younger days I never did
even getting lost for hours.
Didn't want anyone to know I didn't know
where I was going and couldn't read a map
especially her...
I could follow signs...became dependent on them and
strong winds.
Addicted to signage but then came change.
Poor signage, confusing, non existent,
when close, too late, or too small, or
faded with time.
Lost signage, lost my way. I didn't read it right.
I didn't see it coming.
I blame signage.
My way of staying on the map.

Letting Go

Dreams. I had a few.
Wanted to be a cowboy, ride horses
shoot guns, kill bad guys be
the hero of my life.
I had to let go of that.

Wanted to be the quarterback make
touchdowns win exciting games, get the girls,
get lifted up as a
champion all-star.
I had to let go of that.

Wanted to be a great lover, with long
conquest lists, play the field for all it was
worth before finding the most beautiful wife
to be mine forever.
I had to let go of that.

Wanted to be a Hollywood star, admired by
the world, with fan club magazine
covers, the most cheered acceptance
speech for Oscar.
I had to let go of that.

Wanted that perfect family with that perfect wife, perfect gender children, beautiful home in the best neighborhood driving the most expensive car on the block.
I had to let go of that.

Wanted a vacation home, on the lake in the mountains with an inboard motor boat a dock with water sports excellent restaurants nearby and envious neighbors.
I had to let go of that.

Instead

I got to be a respected accountant, an effective lineman, a shy woman-magnet, the president of Kiwanis, owner of a mortgage free home in the nice suburbs, a Subaru, after one divorce, a perfect wife with intelligence and beauty, four unequaled children, two of each, all college graduates, and was voted volunteer of the year when I was 70.

I hold on tight to that.

Trips

Reminds me of early times
when we all were together
having fun impatient wanting to get there
wherever there was then.
We all said it, taking turns, in chorus too
Are we there yet?

Where was there? We picked it then
we had a place to go, we planned the trip, it
was ours, we just didn't want to wait
we made the parents groan to
Are we there yet?

Then came time that made us grow
inside, outside brains and heart
pushed us toward something we didn't know
wondering but never guessing right
Are we there yet?

That commercial on today's TV about a car
that's new, a young writer taking from our
past thinking it funny, cutely retro, dissing
our traditions of family trips sharing, playing,
having fun, wishing to arrive, somewhere
and soon.
Are we there yet?

Now our trips are almost done
with lists that stay uncrossed.
No time left to do it all
try at least for first things first,
as we keep hearing our echoes
from the past
Are we there yet?
And we are.

Solid

Rocks appeal to me
solid to the eye
each itself uncopied
Lined up on the horizontals holding up the
screened-in porch. Can't remember where they
all came from, all over I know that.
I like to try and guess
Oregon and Colorado Wyoming Montana close
to the divide, streams mountains and dried up
river beds, Pocono prizes and Iowa surprizes,
South California with its deserts high and low,
gem mines for tourists on the Blue Ridge Way.
The Eastern shore, north and south
out parcels too, all so them and unexpected.
Colors are their own, with no two shades alike.

Tiny and huge veins wear and tear, rip and
crack, craggy with rough sides showing
however many rains and years expose the
layers breaking off, losing hold, falling down
tumbling to lodge and stay.
Some so smooth from always rushing water
honing the sharp, washing away the years of
being here, going through it all to end up on my
porch. Chips from old mountains,
    leaving me a few leftovers.

Mechanic

Under the spreading china berry tree
saving money and holding court.
Wouldn't touch a dealer with a ten foot pole
rip off, over charge, feigned machine pain for
the %.
Home work, home repairs for all to see
lined up outside running out of room from
folks who want to trust, to get what they pay
for, to drive away pleased.
Young and old gather around like a potbellied
stove from life in a general store
some learn, amazed at the skill, the knowledge
found natural by doing, by listening, by liking.
Some poke fun, offer other ways of theirs,
back when troubles were easier to find, fix and
keep on going, back before life got harder and
machines got smarter
back when that will never come again.

United AME

So quiet it starts. Soft cadenced words of welcome, solemn invitation to the respectful gathering, dressed in finery, mostly, with hats in place, proper suits and ties with sweat soaked shirts. Summer in a smallish church where she lies in state surrounded by flowers, her open face looked upon by a line of friends and curious acquaintances.

The less than accomplished choir with future rock star soloists sing solace and comfort. Prayers begin go on and on others chime in, amen the best, others repeat stamp their feet some jump up begin to yell, shake, make it clear that they feel bad about the death of one so loved.

Ladies in white, almost uniforms, usher make room for those late, pass out programs fans and when prayers come again the final words of praise and glory on high resound to the rafters they nurse the smitten, pass out tissue dry the tears hold up family lest they fall way down into their grief.

Quiet no more with many standing
stretching arms to heaven responding to the
eloquently loud effective leader, his drum beat
repetition gasping for breath crescendoing into
peak until he pulls it back, calms the believers,
brings us back to earth...and then it's done.

She's closed up, taken away, put in the ground
then somewhere else. Emotions spent for
the day, family members depart, stumble,
supported by the stronger friends still wiping
eyes shaking heads wondering when it all
might be for them, then silent relief,
not today.

Desire 76

Standing there, you think you're *sitting*.
Walking, maybe *running*.
Not sure just what it is.
It has your attention. Undivided. For now.
Some days clear and crisp
others cloudy, murky even
but still days, and still there.
Feelings, too. Updown, inout, pushpull
opposites confuse addle but
you don't want it to stop.
If it starts to go you know it.
You can feel it oozing down your leg like waste
you can no longer manage, not sure you want
to. Something else to do.
I never thought it would get so weak
I want it to stay always
yet it cannot. I know I'm losing it.
How about you?

The Edge

Teetering on the edge of tears trying
to balance between what is and what could be,
asking why to all around me. Sadness covers
the living with havings much too small to
measure. Those who could give rewards, even
tokens, to them for being here doing the best
they are able to do with all that load heaved on,
don't. They choose not to see or feel causing
frustrations that grow like open sores and offer
no healing, no smiles to give, no music to dig
out memories of better, very few gifts from
a few finding ways to touch, be present and
move us upward
forward
beyond where we are.

Cultural Exchange
(after seeing a tribute band)

From across the ocean
came those manicured
longhaired liverpoolians
with intent to damage
our youth but changed the world with
I wanna hold your hand seen so mild
today by those who sing instead
I wanna fuck your brains out.
Look how far we've come.

What Happened

Gradually it went away.
We held it up as light, right, the way to be
but slowly at some point in the darkness
new searching lost it
taken by the shallow, the loud, the crude
who didn't think twice, or even once about
what might happen, about how they looked
how they might sound to others
not in that place.
Language raped, laughed at polite, demeaned
meaning and slow sped up to sound levels
rushing ahead of reason, time shrunk to little
left for spending with love, care, concern.
Just I and me deciding fast good or
bad for anyone.
It's hiding somewhere in behind a big safe tree
in an untouched forest waiting to come back
again.

Opportunity

There is a pot of magic that never runs out.
Many rushed to find it knowing
how to use it. Doors were open to the room
where the magic bubbled, those who entered
gathered what they could, not hurried, since
they knew they could return. Others not
yet here were left behind, the chance now
awakened by the stark dark facts of what had
gone before, the sacrifices made by all, that's
all sides of fences, fences built by fear and hate
whose nails, hot from the fire, when heart and
soul got hard, lost all sense of care.
They stick their fingers in the pot, magic for
their few, the ones who stir the stick get first.

What's there to take, but angry touts to let
them know they're mad as hell, treatment is
not fair at least some think that's true.
There are some left who find in fair the core,
what's fair for now a sundown changes, faces
hidden in the night, with dawn some minds are

clearer than had been who know that no one's
right for sure, the stories all are true for them
who see and feel one way not counting hearts
of others.

Magic will not run out. It's always there at
ready. In time perhaps a way will come with
new eyes for the beauty, in time perhaps all
backs will face the crimes out in the street and
four hours lying dead alone will
forever cease to be.

Questions

Picky places under our skin itch
we scratch, festers come
then sores and scabs
blood and more infections
make matters worse
it's all their fault they brought the germs
made a desert of trust, a mockery of hope
a slop jar of love. Everyone knows, you know.
Experts reign giving it all out for free
just ask. Ask the down trod victim how she
feels, ask the cop why he was scared, ask the
lawyer who did what, ask the leader where
he was hiding, ask the mother why her child
talked back, ask the young black man who
made his bed why he ever has to sleep in it.
Let's ask the newsman to tell it right about that
scene he saw last night when those without
simply wanted, but didn't know how to ask,
again.

Fame

A sore throat whisper easy to hear
the touch was almost there
so close moist fingers nearly dripped.
Walking past the gates each day
over many years, got friendly with the keepers
even smiles from time to time, yet only
in a humane way, there were no invitations.
In the back tucked away from crowds
who wanted the same but more, sat the
only one with yeses, given rarely if at all
even if the ache was grounded in much
study, not to mention trying out being told
we don't matter. On the merry go round
reaching for the ring, coming oh so close
each time, still farther than it was, with age
changing what could be, time way out in
front, image growing faint, sounds barely heard
just a memory it becomes but it never
says goodbye.

Hear That

Music will save us. All kinds do.
Nursery rhymes welcome us to a world of love,
piano, strings or toots begin the basic notes
then voices might start to blend in choir and
glee clubs. Desire for better touched by the
muse, lessons start, practice practice practice
to perform or teach or make the notes that
come together in ways that will ease our stress,
make us smile, fall in love, remember when.

Grand symphonic blows our minds, country
ballads break our hearts, Gaga makes us move
our hips, Broadway show tunes remember
time, taps and swan lake enchant the senses.

Makers of the music glow with brilliance given
only them, hearing which will play with what,
give base or treble making whole the melodies
of life that help to give us hope, inspire
encourage to go on finding ways to share it
all, looking always looking for the harmony
binding us like hearts to souls keeping the faith
that tomorrow will only bring us more.

Savings Time

God is all we need. We?
What god, whose god?
Simple those words, those
beliefs that are so old
still here loved as only they can be
by true believers lined up outside
the worship houses not always in them
but always standing firm for a god and son
who came to save a world when
no one knew for sure that it was even lost.

Back then when what was just
a speck known to just a few
they kept it from the rest
to stay the lines drawn in
where they needed them to be.

So remarkable that long ago
grown into our very being
no genius surgeon could remove
the ingested pieces of a life so well told,
lived that no one dare compare.
Beliefs are scattered seeds these days

wind-blown across countless textured fields
taking root as dropped in place
on rich or barren land. Growth will
happen to most we hope and
together find a god...one who might
be the one
since now's the time to save us.

Look Around Some More

Each day to try. Get up.
Take the steps we have to take to get from here
to there, to work, to school,
into the day.
Not always easy, seldom really.
So why do we do it.
Because we have to, need to, can do
will do, to keep it going, to wherever
it is going.
We don't know, though some say so.
We used to believe one or two, until they
looked like the fools they were then no one had
a chance. There is no place of truth.
No book that has it in it. Claims are made
but look at them fighting like mad children,
wanting all or more than them,
not content with some to share.
Who said that's theirs, those have god
who makes the rules for all to hold like
crowns of thorns that prick the skin of color
akin to those across the sand. And in the land
of melting pots with civility at the base not

much better ends of days where efforts are not
strong. Who leads who follows why not both
depending on the whys, one thing's for sure
we have to try the planet needs us trying, two
things for sure we have to try,
just look around, it's dying.

Love Yes

but more is necessary.
respect
at all times
consideration
for all things
admiration
for efforts
cooperation
in tasks
sensitivity
all ways
awareness
in all places
concern
for care
care
for concern
communication
in everything
sharing
mostly
independence
still and
the never to be taken for granted knowledge
that you to each other are together the most
special, most important parts of your lives.

Modern Music 87

Filled up with students in college
to learn new things about the world
how they will fit in it, engage with it
maybe even change it, for the better.
Music lovers mix in well, although most
adults, the highbrow kind, or friends
or relatives of the gifted who on the large
stage employ their skills to give us
pride, wonder and appreciation.
Shostakovich, Tchaikovsky, Rachmaninoff,
Wagner, odd selections for the wind
symphony to offer but still accepted
applauded by those who know how special
each showed that brilliance that lasts.
Odder though was the almost overwhelming
approval shown in the only standing ovation
for a new artist with a new composition
Concerto for Cell Phone. Indication
of new learning and that change for
something better? I was not standing.

Root Cause

Talk about violence,
what causes such, guns
of course, an occasional knife
baseball bats, rocks or other hard
things that produce blunt force
trauma, cut skin and put out eyes.
Objects that can be thrown
across the room, into faces,
belts, coat hangers, wooden paddles,
rat poison, switches called leafless tree
branches, every day uses more than we think.
Rules get broke, some get caught.
Multi shot weapons brought to schools,
taking the lives of many
damaging those who are left. The list is long,
all about *things* that are used.
How about *non-things*, like fists, hands, arms,
feet and perhaps the most vile
of all, words. Guns don't use words
People do. Things don't cause violence.
People do. We do.

Anger

It won't stay down it won't keep quiet
it's always there just lurking
years of reason grown thin with skin
tolerant thoughts are missing
understanding what others do has
long escaped my patience
dumb is dumb, there's no excuse
at least not one I'm thinking
behaviors make my blood boil over
rude and crude with no regrets
my cork pops out juice overflows
I'm embarrassed to admit it
like wiggly worms beneath my skin
who make me shake then tremble
yells burst forth at man and beast
when they keep me from my finding
the truth I think is life for real
the one we should be living yet
I know and madder still it makes me
when I am blamed for being slow
behind the times, can't keep up
get a life you relic.
Quietly once again I suck it up
shut it down and thank them with
I have one.

Will And Testament

A final personal note
Do not have conflict
you know how I felt about that. Indulge me.
Love, patience and understanding please.
Be together even in disagreement, you were
meant to be different but still, be kind, be
considerate. You were all loved very much by
me. Thank you for the gifts of you, and all the
rest you gave.

   I am fine I think from what I think
It was a growing process this time, a lot of
mistakes were made, learned a lot. I hope.
I wish you all strength, awareness, courage,
confidence and clarity as you continue your
journeys. Traveling with you was uniquely ours
and corny special. May you find your way to
peace and may you discover your truths about
these lifetimes. We might see each other again
somewhere sometime, in some form.
We will know it.

Long Enough To Wag

my dog
she needed pushing to move on
to take the step toward staying
she felt my hand on her rear
her tail seemed pleased to feel it

my friends
they looked hard into the face of age daring
it to take them knowing loss, knowing
death refusing to let go
using courage with truthful tongues
that had no need for faking

me
happy to have been here now
for a time that seems so brief
sitting out the dance no more
moving to my beat, time to say
what lives inside, scream it if I must!

About the Author

Jim R. Rogers, born and raised in North Carolina, spent much of his life in Korea, Charlotte, Atlanta, New York, and LA, engaged as a soldier, director, producer, writer in advertising, radio, television, film, and commercial production before changing careers, returning to the Southeast.

He is a UNC Chapel Hill graduate with a master's in early childhood from Coastal Carolina University. Rogers is nationally certified as a family life educator, CFLE, specializing in parenting education, and has been a columnist for over 19 years with the regional newspaper Parent News. He has authored three books, *The Incredible Importance of Effective Parenting,* and free verse poetry *Starts And Stops Along The Way* and his newest book of poems, *Looking Around.* Jim and his partner in life and business, Dr. Sally Z. Hare, are pleased to be the owners of still learning, inc. in Surfside Beach, SC.

<u>For more information</u>
jim@stilllearning.org
www.stilllearning.org

www.ingramcontent.com/pod-product-compliance
Lightning Source LLC
Chambersburg PA
CBHW020111020526
44112CB00033B/1177